FIGHTER PLANES

MARK DARTFORD

Lerner Publications Company
Minneapolis

First American edition published by Lerner Publications Company.

Copyright © 2003 by The Brown Reference Group plc.

Lerner Publications Company.
A division of Lerner Publishing Group
241 First Avenue North
Minneapolis, MN 55401 U.S.A.

Website address: www.lernerbooks.com

Library of Congress Cataloging-in-Publication Data

Dartford, Mark.
 Fighter planes / by Mark Dartford.
     p. cm.—(Military hardware in action)
Includes index.
Summary: An overview of the history and characteristics of fighter
planes.
  ISBN 0–8225–4706–6 (lib. bdg.)
    1. Fighter planes—Juvenile literature. [1. Fighter planes. 2. Airplanes, Military.]
    I. Title. II Series.
  UG1242.F5D3457 2003
  623.7'464—dc21   2002011856

                              √ 6/12/08

Printed in China
Bound in the United States of America
1 2 3 4 5 6 – OS – 08 07 06 05 04 03

This book uses black and yellow chevrons as a decorative element on some headers. They do not point to other elements on the page.

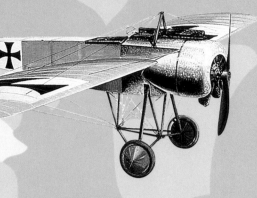

Contents

Introduction

White **vapor trails** twist around the skies as the faint sound of cannon fire reaches the ground. Suddenly, one trail turns to black smoke and spirals down. A combat ends in a kill.

Early Days

From the earliest days, military leaders in several countries took an interest in aviation. Before World War I (1914–1918), airplanes were tested for use in aerial observation. The cavalry worried that noise from aircraft engines would alarm the horses.

BALLOON WARFARE

Balloons had been used for aerial observation in the Civil War (1861–1865). Airplanes could get around more quickly than balloons and could view enemy positions above the range of artillery.

>> **vapor trail** = a condensation track made by aircraft moving through cold ai

World War I

The earliest airplanes that flew over the battlefield in World War I were named scouts. They usually carried a pilot and an observer. When enemy scouts first met in the skies, the observers fired rifles at each other. Later airplanes were fitted with machine guns in the observer's cockpit.

AMERICAN AIRMEN AT WAR

A squadron of U.S. Army Nieuport biplanes (planes with two sets of wings). When the United States joined the war in 1917, Army Air Corps pilots flew French-built Spads and Nieuports.

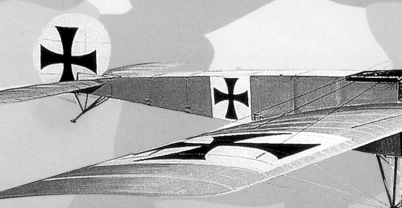

FOKKER SCOURGE

Germany's single-seat Fokker EIII appeared in 1915. It had a machine gun that could fire through the **propeller arc** without hitting the blades. For months, the Fokker ruled the skies over northern France. This period was called the "Fokker Scourge" because the new planes were so deadly and effective.

World War II

By the start of World War II (1939–1945), fast, streamlined, all-metal monoplanes (planes with one set of wings) had replaced most of the biplanes. The new aircraft usually had covered cockpits and wheels that folded up. Machine guns and cannons were fitted into the wings. The new fighter's main task was to protect bombers as they attacked the enemy or to shoot down attacking enemy aircraft and their **fighter escorts.**

THUNDERBOLT

A U.S. P47 Thunderbolt fires its wing guns at night.

>> **fighter escorts** = fighters that protect bombers from attack

Escort Duty

TUSKEGEE AIRMEN

Veteran pilots of the 99th Fighter Squadron and the 332nd Fighter Group pose proudly in front of a restored B25 bomber. Known as the Tuskegee Airmen for their base in Alabama—or as the Red Tails for their distinctive tailplane coloring—the squadron's members were all African Americans. Due to the policy of the time, they were not permitted to join white-only units. On combat escort duties in Europe, the Tuskegee Airmen had an impressive record. They flew 15,000 missions and downed 1,000 German airplanes, without losing a single bomber in their charge.

FRIENDS ABOVE

Vapor trails mark fighters escorting U.S. B17 Flying Fortress bombers over Germany. These fighters were usually P51 Mustangs, equipped with wing **drop tanks** that contained enough fuel to take them to the target and back home again.

The Fighter Role

A fighter's main job is to defend and protect. It keeps the skies free of enemy aircraft by striking them first. Many modern fighters are multirole combat aircraft (MRCA), meaning that they can be used in both defensive and offensive roles.

FIRST JET FIGHTER

In the mid-1940s, Germany's twin-engine Me262 became the first working jet fighter. It could fly higher and faster and could climb more quickly than propeller-driven machines of the time. Although a great combat airplane, it came too late to change the outcome of World War II.

>> **fly-by-wire** = flight controls that operate by computer

CHUCK YAEGER

In 1947 test pilot Chuck Yaeger became the first man to fly faster than the speed of sound. The first jet-on-jet combats occurred during the Korean War (1950–1953). American F86 Sabres tangled with Soviet-built planes over Communist-held North Korea.

TO SOUND AND BEYOND

Supersonic jet fighters are the most important part of a nation's air fleet, with many modern aircraft having multicombat roles. This means they can be adapted for air-to-air combat, ground attack, or bombing tasks.

FIGHTING FALCON

The Lockheed Martin F16 Fighting Falcon is a highly capable all-around fighter and bomber. It has **fly-by-wire** technology and Sidewinder air-to-air missiles on each wing.

DELTA DESIGN

A postwar U.S. Air Force Convair F106 Delta Dart. It was one of the world's first supersonic fighter airplanes.

Combat Air Patrol

In times of political or military tension, the Combat Air Patrol (CAP) is a first line of defense. Like an airborne police patrol, fighters keep watch against intruders. U.S. forces, as well as those of the North Atlantic Treaty Organization (NATO), have regularly flown CAPs in hotspots like Bosnia and the Persian Gulf to enforce United Nations (UN) **no-fly zones.**

EAGLE EYES

A U.S. F15 Eagle on CAP over Bosnia in 1996

>> **no-fly zone** = an area where military flights are banned

Protecting the People

In the international war against air terror, fighter planes play a key role in protecting people and property against attacks. Operation Noble Eagle was mounted after the terror attacks of September 11, 2001, to safeguard U.S. citizens against air terror. A constant combat patrol keeps fighters in the skies 24 hours a day.

ALWAYS ON GUARD

Air National Guard F15s on patrol over New York City

Sight Unseen

The Lockheed-Martin F117 Nighthawk is a twin-engined, single-seat fighter with an attack role. First flown in 1981, the batlike Nighthawk remains at the front of combat aircraft technology. It is coated with a secret radar-absorbing material and is flown with the help of computerized controls. The Nighthawk can strike accurately at enemy defenses without being found by radar. This means that most anti-aircraft weapons are unable to "see" it and therefore will not fire at it.

STEALTHY FIGHTER

The F117 uses **stealth** design to remain invisible to enemy guns and missiles. F117s flew many missions against Iraq and in Bosnia during the 1990s.

>> **stealth** = technology that makes objects invisible to radar

Airborne Warriors

Fighter pilot. The words create the image of a physically fit warrior, fighting alone against a determined opponent. But in the high-tech military environment, teamwork and coordination between air and ground personnel are vital.

sun visor

helmet

oxygen mask

flame-resistant flight suit

survival jacket

flame-resistant gloves

map pocket

pressure suit

rubber soled flying boots

WARRIORS OF THE SKY

A modern fighter pilot is covered from head to toe in flight gear.

FIGHTER PILOTS THROUGH THE AGES

In the open cockpit airplanes of World War I, the aviator wore a thick leather coat, often fur-lined, with a snug leather helmet and goggles to protect against the weather.

>> **G-suit** = a gravity suit that compensates for the effects of high speeds

WORLD WAR II

Fighter pilots in World War II mostly had enclosed cockpits. As their machines flew higher, the pilots needed oxygen masks because of the thin air at high altitudes. They had radio communication, with earphones and a microphone combined in their helmets. They needed warm clothing to cope with the freezing temperatures and life jackets in case of ditching (forced landing in water).

SUPERSONIC AGE

High-altitude fighter pilots have heated **G-suits**. These overalls have special features that balance the loss of blood to the head during high-speed combat moves. A helmet plugged in to the aircraft communications equipment, with a visor to protect against sun glare, is also vital. NASA spacesuit technology has played an important part in flight-suit development.

TEAMWORK

Modern fighter pilots are never alone. They are in constant contact with ground personnel and **air controllers** and with any other aircraft on the same mission. The cockpit is both control room and communications center.

Top Guns

The best fighter pilots, or Top Guns, are selected for their flying ability and for their calmness under pressure. They also need to make decisions quickly and correctly. Above all, pilots must be able to work independently and still be part of a team.

VIRTUAL REALITY

Thanks to modern technology, realistic air battles can be fought in the air, with computer landscapes shown on the aircraft navigation instruments. Large-scale exercises can be practiced high above the ocean, simulating real landscape features below.

FLIGHT TRAINING

Applicants chosen for pilot training begin with small two-seat training aircraft and continue in more advanced trainers like the T38. Modern training also involves many hours of simulated combat on computers, where skills can be learned without risk.

THE INSTRUCTOR

"When you've flown a mission in these simulators, it's a 'been there, done that' sort of thing when it's time for the actual mission."

Instructor, Langley Air Force Base, Virginia

>> **simulator** – a training machine that fakes airplane cockpits and controls

HALL OF FAME

Many fighter pilots have become household names. Baron Manfred von Richthofen, nicknamed the Red Baron, was a top-scoring German ace in World War I. Nearly all of his "kills" were observation airplanes. He attacked from above and behind, a classic fighter technique.

RED BARON

Manfred von Richthofen (*right*) stands with his brother Lothar, also a fighter pilot, in front of his famous Fokker Dr1 Triplane.

"PAPPY" BOYINGTON

Gregory "Pappy" Boyington was the U.S. Marine Corps' top-scoring ace in World War II. He shot down at least 22 enemy planes and later commanded the famous Black Sheep Squadron.

JOHN GLENN JR.

Senator John H. Glenn Jr. was the first astronaut to orbit Earth. As a fighter pilot, he won many medals for bravery. He flew 59 missions in World War II and nearly 100 in the Korean War, shooting down three **MiG**s in nine days of jet combat.

Fighter Weapons

The fighter plane's main task is to find and shoot down enemy aircraft. The planes are armed with air-to-air missiles for long-range fighting and cannons for close combat. Some fighter aircraft are also **fighter-bombers** and are equipped with air-to-ground missiles and bombs.

FULLY LOADED

A Lockheed Martin F16 Fighting Falcon has a full load of wingtip and rack missiles. It also has long-range fuel tanks that can be dropped to lighten the aircraft.

>> **fighter-bomber** = an aircraft that combines fighter and bomber roles

Missiles

Modern fighters carry precision-guided missiles (PGMs). These missiles have guidance systems that steer them onto their target. Most of them are either radar or **infrared guided.**

SIDEWINDER

An F16 firing its wingtip Sidewinder air interception missile (AIM). Sidewinder is one of the longest-serving missiles in the U.S. list and is still one of the most effective. It is infrared guided and has a range of up to 11 miles.

SPARROW

A Navy F/A18 Hornet launches its Sparrow AIM7 radar-guided missile. Like Sidewinder, Sparrow has a long history of development, improvement, and success. It can hit a target over 60 miles away.

Ground Strikers

Many fighters are also MRCAs, airplanes that combine strike capability with aerial combat effectiveness. They are armed with weapons that are guided to their targets by laser or by video. Airplanes like the F4 Phantom and the F16 Fighting Falcon are examples of fighters that can carry ground-attack weapons.

Fighter-Bombers

LASER BOMB

An F4 Phantom drops a precision-guided **laser bomb**. The bomb carries a laser gun in its nose to guide it to its target.

MAVERICK

An F4 Phantom on a low-level attack launches a Maverick air-to-ground missile. The Maverick has an on-board TV camera linked to a cockpit video screen, allowing the pilot to steer it to its target.

>> **laser bomb** = a bomb guided to its target by a laser beam

Guns

In World War II, fighters were equipped only with machine guns or cannons. Most modern fighter airplanes also have cannons, usually high-speed motorized 20mm **Gatling guns**. These are close-range combat weapons. Modern aerial combat relies more on missiles.

BATTLE OF BRITAIN

German Me109s and Royal Air Force (RAF) Spitfires (*top*) fought for control of the skies over England during World War II. These fighters were slower than modern supersonic jets and fought over a smaller area. They were close enough to shoot effectively using just 7.62mm machine guns and 20mm cannons.

CHANGING RANGES

World War II fighter weapons had an effective range of about 500 yards. World War I aircraft had half that range. By comparison, some modern fighter missiles can engage targets well over 100 miles away.

>> **Gatling gun** = a chain-driven aircraft cannon with a high rate of fire

Fighters in Action

Nearly a century of aerial conflict separates the dogfights of World War I from modern long-distance, high-tech missile exchanges. Pilots and machines have changed, but the basic goal remains the same: defending the skies from enemy intruders.

World War II

When the U.S. Army Air Force (USAAF) began sending bombers to Germany, the large, slow planes were easy targets for the fast German fighters. The U.S. bombers were shot down at an alarming rate. The P51D Mustang was introduced as a long-range escort fighter. It was able to follow and protect the bombers deep in enemy territory, saving the lives of many bomber crews. The U.S. **attrition rate** soon went down.

KEEPING WATCH

Long-range P51 Mustangs keep a lookout for enemy fighters as they escort a formation of USAAF B17 heavy bombers on a daylight raid over Germany in 1944.

>> **attrition rate** – military term for losses of personnel or equipment

MIGHTY MUSTANG

The North American P51 Mustang was an outstanding World War II fighter. It was originally built for the RAF. Early versions did not perform well at high altitudes, so the Mustang was refitted with a Rolls Royce Merlin engine. This combination resulted in the most successful fighter program in history. Starting in 1941, more than 15,000 P51s were built, and many are still flying.

Details:
Crew: 1
Length: 33 ft.
Wingspan: 37 ft.
Propulsion: 1 x 1590 hp Merlin
Max Speed: 437 mph
Ceiling: 42,000 ft.
Armament: 6 x 0.5 in. Browning machine guns

MAKING HISTORY

"The Mustang was pleasant and forgiving to fly ... We sensed it was special, even before we measured it against what the enemy pilots were flying."

Clarence "Bud" Anderson,
P51 fighter ace

"The day I saw Mustangs over Berlin, I knew the game was up."

Hermann Goering,
Hitler's deputy and commander in chief of the German air force

D DAY MUSTANG

A P51 Mustang in high-visibility **D day** stripes for easy identification.

Fighters in Action

The first jet fighter clashes took place during the Korean War. After Communist North Korea, with support from China, invaded South Korea, the United States and the UN responded. North American F86 Sabres fought against Soviet-built MiG15s for control of the skies over the Yalu River, an area that became known as "MiG Alley."

UN FORCES RETREAT

UN forces pull back across the **38th Parallel** following the Communist invasion in 1950.

SABRES RULE

An F86 Sabre. The MiG versus Sabre contests matched up the era's two best fighters. North Korea lost 792 MiGs to the loss of 78 Sabres. The air war was won, and the Communists retreated.

In 1981 tension between democratic nations and the Mediterranean nation of Libya were at their height. Libyan leader Muammar El-Qaddafi extended the country's territorial claim over the Mediterranean Sea from 2 to 12 miles, breaking international law. U.S. aircraft carriers sailed in to stop Libya from staking its claim.

Dogfight with Libya

TOMCAT REVENGE

A carrier-based Grumman F14 Tomcat

On August 19, 1981, two F14 Tomcats were flying a CAP in the skies near Libya in North Africa. Two Libyan Su22s approached, and one fired its **Atoll** missile. The missile failed, and the Tomcats attacked. The F14s shot down both SU22s using AIM9 Sidewinders. In 1989, in a similar incident, F14s took out two Libyan MiG23s.

Falklands War

In 1982 Argentine forces invaded the Falkland Islands off the Argentine coast. Argentina resented British ownership of the islands, and its military government faced public unrest. Argentina's taking of the islands from the small Royal Marines unit gained popular support in Argentina. Britain responded by sending ships, planes, and troops to the area. Argentine forces surrendered in July 1982.

HARRIER AT WAR

The Hawker Sea Harrier (the British version of the AV8 jump jet) was the only aircraft able to fly from the short decks of the Royal Navy's **VSTOL** carriers. RAF and Royal Navy pilots flew a total of 1,435 missions against Argentine targets during the two-month conflict. They shot down at least 20 planes, with no losses of their own.

Desert Storm

During the 1991 Persian Gulf War against Iraq, U.S. and **Coalition** fighter forces flew a number of missions. The 58th Fighter Squadron, part of the 33rd Fighter Wing based at Eglin Air Force Base, Florida, was one of the units that served with success.

FAR FROM HOME

A 58th Tactical Fighter Squadron F15 Eagle over the Iraqi desert in 1991.

RISKY BUSINESS

"There are pilots and there are pilots; with the good ones, it is inborn. You can't teach it. If you are a fighter pilot, you have to be willing to take risks."

General Robin Olds, U.S. Air Force

MIG DOWN

An Iraqi pilot ejects from his destroyed MiG. On January 17, 1991, Captain John Kelk scored the first air-to-air victory by shooting down a Russian-built Iraqi MiG29. The 58th Fighter Squadron destroyed five MiG29s, more any other squadron during the five-week air war.

Fighter Tactics

A fighter plane is only as good as the pilot who flies it. The pilot relies on training and proven methods of attack. Nearly a century of air warfare has produced fighting tactics that in some cases go back to World War I.

Golden Rules

Attack from above and behind; watch for attackers against the sun; keep searching the sky. All these basic air combat laws date back to World War I, when aviation created a new kind of warfare.

KNOW WHERE YOU ARE

A fighter pilot must keep continuous lookout and not be confused by making high-speed moves.

>> **flying circus** = a World War I term for a large group of airplanes

FORMATIONS

F16 Flying Falcons in a tight V formation. Most formations are made up of combinations of aircraft in twos or threes. The pilots on the leader's wings keep a defensive watch, while the leader seeks out the enemy. Other formations include finger four, line abreast, and line astern.

SAFETY IN NUMBERS

Large **flying circuses** and "wings" were a feature of both world wars. Dozens of airplanes, all flying in **formation,** were a powerful anti-enemy force. The downside was the length of time it sometimes took to gather so many machines at a time.

EYES ALL AROUND

In the finger four formation, adopted in World War II, a section of four aircraft each guards a portion of the sky.

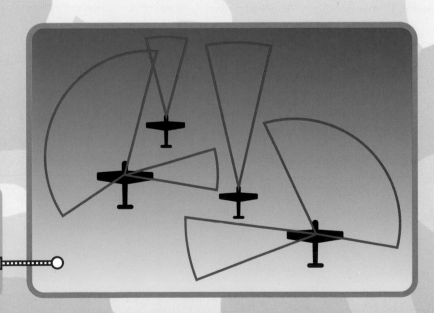

Fighter Tactics

In modern warfare, the airplane that has the tightest turning circle (the diameter of a 360 degree turn) has an advantage. It can always turn out of an attacker's line of fire. With precision-guided missile technology, the turn is less important. But ease of movement can still outsmart a missile.

HARRIER JUMP JET

The jump jet can perform maneuvers that no other type of fighter can match. It uses its **vectored thrust nozzles** to skip out of its flight path. This tactic is known as "viffing," for vectoring-in-flight. This Harrier (*top*) is thrusting away from its Sepecat Jaguar wingman.

ELECTRONIC WARFARE

Most modern air-to-air contacts rely on technology to identify and strike a target. The enemy may be beyond visual range but can be targeted by radar. Precision guided "fire and forget" missiles can then **lock-on**, traveling at speeds of Mach 4 (four times the speed of sound, about 2500 mph).

>> **vectored thrust nozzles** – rotating jetpipes, for vertical takeoff

A Navy F/A18 Hornet crashes through the sound barrier in a burst of vapor. The greatest advantage any fighter plane has is its speed, both in attack and in defense.

ALWAYS TRUE

"The most important thing to a fighter pilot is speed. The faster an aircraft is moving when he spots the enemy, the sooner he will be able to take the bounce .... It's like sneaking up behind someone with a baseball bat."

Duane W. Beeson, P51 Mustang pilot, 1945

Fighter Enemies

Fighters can be shot down by other airplanes or by surface-launched missiles. They are also at risk from radar-guided anti-aircraft guns. Apart from speed and pilot skill, modern jet fighters are also equipped with defensive technology.

DOG EATS DOG

An Israeli **Mirage** (*below*) sweeps past its victim, an Egyptian Su7, during the 1973 **Yom Kippur War**. Speeds and distances have increased over the years, and missiles have replaced machine guns and cannons. But another fighter is still a fighter's number-one enemy.

MACH 5 MISSILES

U.S. Navy crewmembers prepare to load a Phoenix missile onto an F14 Tomcat. Because many fighters can travel at more than twice the speed of sound, air-to-air missiles have to be even faster. The Phoenix AIM54 reaches a speed of Mach 5, with a range of well over 100 miles.

>> **Mirage** = a supersonic fighter and strike airplane built in France

From the Ground Up

Missiles launched from the ground or from warships at sea are another hazard, especially to low-flying aircraft.

TRIPLE A

U.S. Marines fill the night sky with anti-aircraft fire during a Japanese raid on a U.S. airbase during World War II. Anti-aircraft artillery is most effective against low-level fighter-bomber attacks.

Fighter Enemies

Ground-based radar stations are the first line of defense against fighter or bomber intruders. Radar was first used to find approaching enemy airplanes during World War II. The British used radio direction finding, as it was then called, to pick up enemy aircraft in 1940, during the Battle of Britain.

ALWAYS WATCHING

Modern detection systems are highly sophisticated. They use both radar and satellite technology to give **ground controllers** early and accurate information about incoming air threats.

Defensive Arsenal

The modern fighter aircraft has the ability to defend itself against attackers. Electronic countermeasures (ECM) make up a package of technology that finds and stops enemy action. Onboard radar can find out when an enemy missile has locked-on. The radar either jams the missile's homing signals or confuses it by sending out flares.

SIGHT IS MIGHT

"One of the secrets of air fighting was to see the other first. Seeing airplanes from great distances was a question of training and experience, of knowing where to look and what to look for...."

Air Vice-Marshal "Johnnie" Johnson, Royal Air Force

SEE AND EVADE

Even with a cockpit full of electronics, the fighter pilot personally plays a part in the flight. Constant visual scanning is part of the pilot's defensive arsenal. A telltale vapor streak in the sky can mean an attacking airplane or a **homing missile**.

>> **homing missile** = a guided missile using radar or infrared target finding

Fighters

Fighter aircraft are the first defense against enemy airborne attack. The planes are fast and comparatively small. Just one or sometimes two pilots make up the crew. Fighters and those who fly them are the best of the best in the air.

F16 FIGHTING FALCON

The Lockheed Martin F16 Fighting Falcon was introduced as a smaller and cheaper version of the F15 Eagle. It has since performed well as both a fighter and a fighter-bomber in combat and in advanced training roles.

Details:
Crew: 1
Length: 30 ft.
Wingspan: 47 ft. 7 in.
Propulsion: 1 x 24,000 lb. thrust **turbofan**
Max Speed: 1,300 mph
Ceiling: 60,000 ft.
Armament: 1 x 20mm cannon, 15,200 lb. **external load**

F15 EAGLE

The McDonnell Douglas F15 is a fighter specifically developed to meet the threat thought to come from the Soviet Union's MiG23s and MiG25s. There is a dual-seat advanced-trainer version (*shown*) and a single-seat combat model.

Details:
Crew: 1–2
Length: 63 ft.
Wingspan: 42 ft. 9 in.
Propulsion: 2 x 23,800 lb. thrust turbofan
Max Speed: 1,650 mph
Ceiling: 70,000 ft.
Armament: 1 x 20mm cannon, 12,000 lb. external load

F4 PHANTOM

The McDonnell Douglas F4 is one of the world's all-time great combat aircraft. Rugged and adaptable, it has seen active service with air forces across the world for several decades. As a land-based fighter-bomber and carrier-based fighter, it has an outstanding record.

Details:
Crew: 2
Length: 58 ft. 3 in.
Wingspan: 38 ft. 5 in. (spread)
Propulsion: 2 x 20,515 lb. thrust afterburning turbofans
Max Speed: 1,500 mph
Ceiling: 60,000 ft.
Armament: 1 x 20mm cannon, 16,000 lb. external load

>> **external load** = weapons or equipment carried on wing or fuselage racks

Fighters

SU27 "FLANKER"

Dubbed "Flanker" by NATO, the Sukhoi 27 is a Russian-built **air-superiority fighter** like the F15 Eagle. There is a carrier-based version, the Su33, and a two-seat, side-by-side strike model, the Su34.

Details:
Crew: 1
Length: 71 ft. 9 in.
Wingspan: 48 ft.
Propulsion: 2 x 27,557 lb. thrust afterburning turbofan
Max Speed: 1,555 mph at altitude
Ceiling: 59,000 ft.
Armament: 1 x 30mm cannon, bombs, and air-to-air missiles

MIG29 "FULCRUM"

The MiG29 "Fulcrum" is a Russian-built all-weather fighter and strike airplane that can carry **nuclear warheads.** It has a helmet-mounted line-of-sight weapon system that steers its missiles where the pilot looks. It compares with the F/A18 and the F15.

Details:
Crew: 1
Length: 56 ft. 10 in.
Wingspan: 36 ft. 5 in.
Propulsion: 2 x 22,200 lb. thrust turbofan
Max Speed: 1,520 mph
Ceiling: 60,000 ft.
Armament: 1 x 30mm cannons, variable missile load

>> **air-superiority fighter** – an airplane designed to knock out any opposition

SU37 "TERMINATOR"

The all-weather Sukhoi 37 is easy to fly and is the multirole fighter version of the Su27. It is Russia's most advanced fighting airplane. It has fully digitized fly-by-wire controls.

Details:
Crew: 1
Length: 72 ft.
Wingspan: 49 ft. 9 in.
Propulsion: 2 x 30,855 lb. vectored-thrust afterburning turbofans
Max Speed: 1,516 mph
Ceiling: 59,000 ft.
Armament: 1 x 30mm cannon, 18,075 lb. bomb and/or missile load

Fighters

MIRAGE 2000

The Dassault-Breguet Mirage 2000 is a combat-proven fighter-interceptor built in France. The Mirage delta-wing fighter, one of the most technically advanced combat aircraft in the world, is in service with air forces in many countries.

Details:
Crew: 1
Length: 50 ft. 3 in.
Wingspan: 29 ft. 5 in.
Propulsion: 1 x 15,873 lb. thrust afterburning turbofan
Max Speed: 1,450 mph
Ceiling: 50,000 ft.
Armament: 2 x 30mm cannons, 8,820 lb. ordnance load

SEPECAT JAGUAR

The Jaguar is a joint French and British fighter-bomber. The fighter version is equipped with twin cannons and **ASRAAM** (short-range air-to-air missiles). The strike version is in use with several other countries, including India and Oman, and can be adapted to carry nuclear weapons.

Details:
Crew: 1
Length: 55 ft. 2 in.
Wingspan: 28 ft. 6 in.
Propulsion: 2 x 7305 lb. thrust afterburning
   turbofans
Max Speed: 900 mph
Ceiling: 40,000 ft.
Armament: 1 x 30mm Arden cannon,
   10,000 lb. **ordnance** load

JAS39 GRIPEN

The JAS39 Gripen (Griffin) is built by Saab Military Industries, a Swedish world leader in combat aircraft design. The Gripen is a compact multirole fighter with air defense and strike capabilities.

Details:
Crew: 1
Length: 46 ft. 3 in.
Wingspan: 27 ft. 7 in.
Propulsion: 1 x 18,100 lb. thrust
afterburning
   turbofan
Max Speed: 1,321 mph
Ceiling: 50,000 ft.
Armament: 1 x 27mm Mauser cannon,
   14,330 lb. bomb and missile load

Fighters

A7 CORSAIR II

The Vought Corsair II was one of the longest-serving carrier-based aircraft flown by the U.S. Navy. Corsairs saw action in Vietnam in the 1960s and against Libyan terrorist targets in the 1980s. After two decades of service, the airplane was replaced by the F/A18 Hornet.

Details:
Crew: 1
Length: 46 ft.
Wingspan: 38 ft. 9 in.
Propulsion: 1 x 11,350 lb. thrust turbofans
Max Speed: 645 mph at patrol level
Ceiling: 35,000 ft.
Armament: 1 x 20mm cannon, 20,000 lb. ordnance load

F14 TOMCAT

The Grumman F14 Tomcat is a supersonic all-weather interceptor with **variable geometry wings.** It is the U.S. Navy's most advanced fighter plane and can track up to 24 aircraft at one time. The F14 was designed as a replacement for the F4 Phantom.

Details:
Crew: 2
Length: 61 ft. 9 in.
Wingspan: 64 ft. unswept
Propulsion: 2 x 20,900 lb. thrust afterburning turbofans
Max Speed: 1,564 mph
Ceiling: 53,000 ft.
Armament: 1 x 20mm cannon, 14,500 lb. bomb and missile load

F5 TIGER II

The Northrop F5 is a small fighter and advanced trainer that has a history dating back to the 1950s. Lightweight and reliable, its flight advantages (similar to the Russian MiG21) have led to its adoption as an enemy aircraft simulator for combat training.

Details:
Crew: 1
Length: 48 ft. 2 in.
Wingspan: 26 ft. 8 in.
Propulsion: 2 x 5000 lb. thrust afterburning **turbojets**
Max Speed: 640 mph at sea level
Ceiling: 51,800 ft.
Armament: 2 x 20mm cannons, 5000 lb. ordnance load

>> **turbojet** = a jet engine with rotating blades to increase airflow and power

Fighters of the Future

The next generation of combat aircraft will be faster, easier to move around, and better equipped than current frontline fighters. The emphasis will be on stealth and on more accurate and harder-hitting missile systems.

ENTER THE RAPTOR

The F22 Raptor, developed by Boeing and Lockheed Martin, is set to replace the F15 Eagle air-superiority fighter. It will become operational with U.S. and allied air forces and navies during the first decade of the twenty-first century. The F22 will combine stealth design with supersonic ease of movement. Its state-of-the-art target-finding and missile delivery systems will make the Raptor the world leader for many years.

>> **airframe** = a structural part of an airplane, like a skeleton

X-Planes Explained

X31 ENHANCED MANEUVERABILITY DEMONSTRATOR

The X31 tests thrust-vectoring techniques. Many airplanes are developed just to try out different **airframes** or technology and never go to full-scale manufacture. In the United States, these are known as X-Planes and are tested in great secrecy at places like the famous Lockheed Martin "Skunk Works" at Edwards Air Force Base in California. Stealth and variable geometry are two examples of the technology resulting from these trials. These tests give U.S. manufacturers a cutting edge in future fighter production.

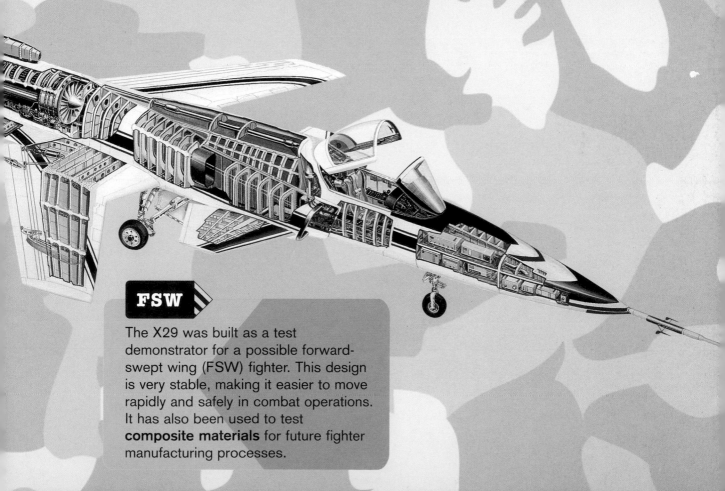

FSW

The X29 was built as a test demonstrator for a possible forward-swept wing (FSW) fighter. This design is very stable, making it easier to move rapidly and safely in combat operations. It has also been used to test **composite materials** for future fighter manufacturing processes.

Fighters of the Future

European manufacturers have spent many years working together on joint fighter aircraft for the twenty-first century. The Eurofighter and the Rafale are two examples that are reaching production stage and will equip several NATO countries in Europe, as well as their allies worldwide.

EUROFIGHTER

"Designed by pilots for pilots" is the scoop on the multirole Eurofighter. Germany, Britain, Spain, Italy, and France have all contributed to the program over three decades. It will be a low-cost, high-speed interceptor, with additional strike capability.

>> **cruise missile** – a guided missile that flies at low level to its target

RAFALE

France developed the Dassault Rafale to enlarge and replace its existing Mirage and Super Etendard fleets. Rafale can carry more than 13,000 pounds of ordnance, including the French ASMP nuclear **cruise missile**.

F35

The U.S. military has chosen the Lockheed Martin F35 over the Boeing F32 project as its **joint strike** airplane with a secondary interceptor capability. In addition to ground strike ordnance, it will have air-to-air interception missiles and machine guns for aerial combat. It will support—and one day replace—the F16 Fighting Falcon and the F/A18 Hornet.

>> **joint strike** = a strike airplane with added fighter capability

Hardware at a Glance

AA = anti-aircraft

AIM = air interception missile

ASRAAM = advanced short-range air-to-air missile

CAP = combat air patrol

ECM = electronic countermeasures

FSA = Future Strike Aircraft

FSW = forward swept wing

GPS = Global Positioning System

JDAM = Joint Direct Attack Munition

JSF = Joint Strike Fighter

MRCA = multirole combat aircraft

NASA = National Aeronautics and Space Administration

NATO = North Atlantic Treaty Organization

PGM = precision-guided missile

VSTOL = vertical or short takeoff and landing

Further Reading & Websites

Angelucci, Enzo. *The Illustrated Encyclopedia of Military Aircraft.* New York: Book Sales, 2001.

Berliner, Don. *Stealth Fighters and Bombers.* Berkeley Heights, NJ: Enslow Publishing, 2001.

Chant, Christopher. *Early Fighters (The World's Greatest Aircraft).* Broomall, PA: Chelsea House, 1999.

Chant, Christopher. *The Role of the Fighter & Bomber.* Broomall, PA: Chelsea House, 1999.

Emert, Phyllis Raybin. *Fighter Planes (Wild Wings Series).* New York: Julian Messner, 1990.

Graham, Ian. *Attack Fighters (Designed for Success).* New York: Heinemann, 2003

Holden, Henry M. *Air Force Aircraft (Aircraft).* Berkeley Heights, NJ: Enslow Publishing, 2001.

Holden, Henry M. *Navy Combat Aircraft and Pilots (Aircraft).* Berkeley Heights, NJ: Enslow Publishing, 2002.

Jenssen, Hans. *Look Inside Cross-Sections: Jets.* New York: DK Publishing, 1996.

Loves, June. *Military Aircraft (Flight).* Broomall, PA: Chelsea House, 2001.

Norman, C.J. *Combat Aircraft.* London: Franklin Watts, 1990.

Rendall, David. *Jane's Aircraft Recognition Guide.* New York: HarperCollins, 1999.

Spick, Mike. *B1B (Modern Fighting Aircraft, Vol 11).* New York: Simon & Schuster,1986.

Taylor, Mike. *Air Forces of World War II (World War II).* Edina, MN: Abdo & Daughters, 1998.

Air Force Link <http://www.af.mil>

Blue Angels <http://www.navyjobs.com/blueangels/>

Center of Military History <http://www.army.mil/cmh-pg>

Commemorative Air Force <http://www.commemorativeairforce.org>

Federation of American Scientists <http://www.fas.org/man.index.html>

Fighter Planes <http://www.fighter-planes.com>

Military History Online <http://www.militaryhistoryonline.com>

NATO multimedia <http://www.nato.int>

U.S. Marine Corps <http://www.usmc.mil>

U.S. Navy <http://www.navy.mil>

Places to Visit

You can see examples of some of the fighters and combat airplanes contained in this book by visiting the military museums listed here.

American Airpower Heritage Museum, Midland, TX <www.airpowermuseum.org>
Army Aviation Museum, Fort Rucker, Ozark, AL <www.armyavnmuseum.org>
Canadian Warplane Heritage Museum, Hamilton Airport, Mount Hope, Ontario
   <www.warplane.com>
Kenosha Military Museum, Pleasant Prairie, WI <www.kenoshamilitarymuseum.com>
Mighty Eighth Air Force Heritage Museum, Pooler, GA <www.mighty8thmuseum.com>
National Museum of Naval Aviation, Pensacola, FL <www.naval-air.org>
Old Rhinebeck Aerodrome, Rhinebeck, NY <www.oldrhinebeck.org>
RCAF Memorial Museum, Trenton, Ontario <www.rcafmuseum.on.ca>
San Diego Aerospace Museum, San Diego, CA <www.aerospacemuseum.org>
Smithsonian National Air and Space Museum, Washington, DC <www.nasm.si.edu>
U.S. Air Force Museum, Wright-Patterson AFB, OH <www.wpafb.af.mil/museum/>
Valiant Air Command Warbird Museum, Titusville, FL <www.vacwarbirds.org>
War Eagles Air Museum, Santa Teresa, NM <www.war-eagles-air-museum.com>
Western Canada Aviation Museum, Winnipeg, Manitoba <www.wcam.mb.ca>

Index

Picture Sources

Autowrite; 27
BAe; 14, 38, 44
Corel; 9 (b), 19 (t), 41
Dassault; 39 (b), 45 (t)
Defense Visual Information Center; 4 (b), 5 (t), 6, 13,
16–17, 17, 18, 22, 23, 24, 25, 26, 27, 30, 31, 35 (b),
40–41
John Batchelor; 5 (b), 9 (c), 21, 42–43

M K Dartford; 4 (t), 12 (r), 28, 36–37, 39 (t)
Embraer;
Robert Hunt Library; 7 (b), 12 (l), 15 (t), 20
U.S. Air Force; 7 (t), 8, 9 (t), 10, 11 (t), 11 (b), 32, 33
(b), 34, 35 (t), 42, 45
U.S. Army;
U.S. Marine Corps; 15 (b)
U.S. Navy; 29, 33 (t), 40, 43